W9-BRH-141

Presented to

Shannon Crouch

By

Lynn Grimsley
"Grims" ☺Л

Date

5/17/05

LIFE AFTER HIGHSCHOOL

TH1NK
™

Go Ahead:

TH1NK: *about God*
about life
about others

Faith isn't just an act; it's something you live—something huge and sometimes unimaginable. By getting into the real issues in your life, TH1NK books open opportunities to talk honestly about your faith, your relationship with God and others, as well as all the things life throws at you.

Don't let other people th1nk for you . . .

TH1NK for yourself.

www.th1nkbooks.com

LIFE AFTER **HIGHSCHOOL**
GOD'S ADVICE FOR GRADS

FEATURING THE MESSAGE//REMIX

TH1NK Books
an imprint of NavPress®

TH1NK
P.O. Box 35001
Colorado Springs, Colorado 80935

TH1NK is an imprint of NavPress.

ISBN 1-57683-522-7

Cover design by BURNKIT
Cover image by Joshua Dunford Photography
Creative Team: Sarah Snelling, Gabe Filkey (s.c.m.), Jim Lund, Darla Hightower, Pat Miller

Life after high school : God's advice for grads.
    p. cm.
 ISBN 1-57683-522-7
 1. High school graduates--Prayer-books and devotions--English. 2.
High school graduates--Conduct of life. I. NavPress (Firm)
 BV4850.L54 2005
 248.8'4--dc22

                2004021292

Printed in Canada

1 2 3 4 5 / 09 08 07 06 05

FOR A FREE CATALOG OF
NAVPRESS BOOKS & BIBLE STUDIES,
CALL 1-800-366-7788 (USA)
OR 1-416-499-4615 (CANADA)

CONTENTS

OWNING MY FAITH

WET CEMENT

Life after high school is a little like wet cement. You've already poured that gooey mixture of your ideals, the things you believe in, who you're going to become, and what you're going to live for into a "frame," but the project is far from finished. It hasn't settled. You need time to shape it, smooth it out, and discover exactly what it's going to look like. And you're really hoping you'll still recognize it when it's done.

The post–high school life is like wet cement in another way — a lot of people will leave an imprint on who you are. In a world that's continually bombarding you with new ideas, new demands, and data you "need" to know, it's not always easy to decide which imprints to smooth over and which ones to let stick. Nearly every day brings a fresh challenge or crisis. You may be facing more questions than you know what to do with—and too few answers.

Yet there is a constant amid the madness: God. He's been there through all of your triumphs and disasters to this point, and He'll still be there tomorrow. He sees exactly who you are—and loves you for being that person. He also has a life in mind for you that's better than your best dreams: "I know what I'm doing. I have it all planned out—plans to take care of you, not abandon you, plans to give you the future you hope for" (Jeremiah 29:11).

Life After High School can help you discover that future. This book is a tool; it's not meant to replace reading the Bible, and it's not meant to be read without a Bible. It's made up of thirty questions designed to help you deal with life *today*, right where you are. Each question is followed by text that will take you deeper, critical advice from God that's presented in the everyday language of *The Message*, and more questions and material that are guaranteed to make you think.

There's that word again: *think*. In the days and years ahead, you'll find your brain and your beliefs being tested in ways you never imagined. Worried about cracks in the cement that forms your life? Choose to let God handle the finishing touches. You're sure to like what He comes up with.

KNOWING GOD

LOVE

With all the people in the world, how do I know God really loves me?

Have you ever seen the birth of a human baby? The mother usually arrives at the hospital filled with feelings of excitement and anticipation. As the minutes turn into hours, however, tension and unspoken worries arise: *Is everything proceeding normally? Is my baby going to be okay?* You watch pain contort her face during the contractions and wonder why anyone would *ever* want to go through this. But then comes the moment all have been waiting for. You can see it in Mom's eyes the moment she locks onto that precious newborn—an unmistakable combination of joy, relief, and love.

God's love for each of us—for *you*—is something

like that. In fact, even more so. After all, He created and "birthed" you, with your unique characteristics, talents, and gifts specifically in mind. He knows you better than you know yourself, right down to the number of hairs on your head (see Matthew 10:30). He's waiting for you to discover the plans He has for you. He *chose* you. Most incredible of all, He sacrificed His own Son so that you could live forever with Him. *That's* love!

John wrote, "Everyone who confesses that Jesus is God's Son participates continuously in an intimate relationship with God. We know it so well, we've embraced it heart and soul, this love that comes from God" (1 John 4:15-16). Even with six billion people in the world, God's love is big enough to cover each of us individually. He *is* love (see 1 John 4:16), and He's ready to overwhelm you with that love if you'll only open up your arms—and your heart.

GOD'S ADVICE

This is how God showed his love for us: God sent his only Son into the world so we might live through him.

1 JOHN 4:9

You know me inside and out, you know every bone in my body; you know exactly how I was made, bit by bit, how I was sculpted from nothing into something.

PSALM 139:15

You are the ones chosen by God.

1 PETER 2:9

"If someone has a hundred sheep and one of them wanders off, doesn't he leave the ninety-nine and go after the one? And if he finds it, doesn't he make far more over it than over the ninety-nine who stay put? Your Father in heaven feels the same way.

MATTHEW 18:12-14

First we were loved, now we love. [God] loved us first.

1 JOHN 4:19

Do you think anyone is going to be able to drive a wedge between us and Christ's love for us? There is no way! Not trouble, not hard times, not hatred, not hunger, not homelessness, not bullying threats, not backstabbing, not even the worst sins listed in Scripture. . . . None of this fazes us because Jesus loves us.

ROMANS 8:35-37

Love

KNOWING GOD

REALITY CHECK

○ Do you ever doubt God's love for you as an individual? Why?

○ Do you believe you could ever make God not love you?

○ What does it mean to be "chosen" by God?

○ How would your life change if you were fully aware of God's love for you on a moment-by-moment basis?

Prayer

Lord, I do believe that You love each of Your creations—even me. Help me to see and truly understand that nothing can stand in the way of Your love. Thank You for allowing Your Son, Jesus, to give up His life for me. Enable me to open up my heart and soul so that I can experience Your amazing love every moment of every day. I love you! Amen.

SALVATION

Would God send my friends to hell?

Hell. Not the most comfortable dinner topic. You probably won't see, "What's for dessert? And by the way, what do you think about eternal damnation?" on anyone's list of sure-fire conversation starters. But that little matter of where you and your closest friends will spend forever *is* significant. It's the whole reason God took human form and died for us (see John 3:16).

You may not be thrilled about the idea of invading others' comfort zone to talk about their salvation, least of all your friends. You may wonder if it's necessary. God will take care of it, right? Well, it's true that God loves each of us deeply. He doesn't *want* to condemn anyone.

As Peter said, "[God] is restraining himself on account of you, holding back the End because he doesn't want anyone lost. He's giving everyone space and time to change" (2 Peter 3:9). But God leaves the decision entirely in our hands. He honors us that way. Though He persistently pursues us, employing every imaginable method to encourage us to repent and believe, He will not force us. For better — "whoever believes and is baptized is saved" (Mark 16:16) — or for worse — "whoever refuses to believe is damned" (verse 16) — it's a choice that each of us makes.

It's also true that nearly everyone knows of and has formed an opinion on God. Paul said that "nobody has a good excuse" for ignoring the truth about Him (Romans 1:18-20). Like everyone else, your friends are heading one way or the other — to a forever future with the Father or a forever nightmare with the Devil. So even if the subject isn't comfortable, it may be time to speak up. Your friends will be eternally grateful.

GOD'S ADVICE

"This is how much God loved the world: He gave his Son, his one and only Son. And this is why: so that no one need by destroyed; by believing in him, anyone can have a whole and lasting life."

JOHN 3:16

The basic reality of God is plain enough. Open your eyes and there it is! By taking a long and thoughtful look at what God has created, people have always been able to see what their eyes as such can't see: eternal power, for instance, and the mystery of his divine being. So nobody has a good excuse.

ROMANS 1:19-20

"Go everywhere and announce the Message of God's good news to one and all. Whoever believes and is baptized is saved; whoever refuses to believe is damned."

MARK 16:15-16

"Anyone who trusts in him is acquitted; anyone who refuses to trust him has long since been under the death sentence without knowing it. And why? Because of that person's failure to believe in the one-of-a-kind Son of God when introduced to him.

JOHN 3:18

[Jesus] asked him, "Do you believe in the Son of Man?" The man said, "Point him out to me, sir, so that I can believe in him." Jesus said, "You're looking right at him. . . ." "Master, I believe," the man said, and worshiped him.

JOHN 9:35-38

Salvation

KNOWING GOD

REALITY CHECK

◯ Is God fair? Why or why not?

◯ Do you know where your friends stand regarding their salvation?

◯ How easy is it for you to discuss heaven and hell with the people you hang out with?

◯ How has God encouraged you to find Him?

◯ Why do you think God allows us to choose our destiny?

The Next Step

Choose a friend who may not have turned over his life to Jesus. Pray for him. Think about ways you might talk to him about his salvation. Then pick a day and time to approach him and follow through. Let God guide you in your conversation.

WORSHIP

Think back to your last concert. You bought your tickets weeks before, then waited in line for hours to jam into a stadium with thousands of fans. The opening act has finished. Now the lights are low. The bass thumps in anticipation. The music builds. This is the moment you've been waiting for! Finally, a single spotlight hits the stage, revealing the star performer as he launches into your favorite song. The crowd explodes in a joyful mix of cheering, dancing, and singing.

There's a thrill that comes with this kind of experience, whether it's at a concert, a political rally, or a football game. It fills a very tangible need inside each of us.

The reason is that we were *created to worship*. In one form or another, we all revere something. If it's not the fame and talent of others, it's money and the things it buys, the status that comes from education and career success, or physical beauty. New agers will tell us that *we* are God, leading to a kind of self-worship. Only the wise realize that none of these things satisfies in the end. God makes the true purpose of worship clear: "The people I made especially for myself, a people custom-made to praise me" (Isaiah 43:21).

Worship comes in many forms: words and shouts of praise, singing, dancing, quiet meditation. Even the way that we live is a type of worship that pleases God. It isn't the style that's important, but our consistency and sincerity. The object of our worship is important to God—He made it the focus of His first two commandments—because it reflects our priorities, who we belong to, and who we're becoming. When we worship God, we move that much closer to Him and to our destiny.

GOD'S ADVICE

I am GOD, your God, who brought you out of the land of Egypt, out of a life of slavery. No other gods, only me. No carved gods of any size, shape, or form of anything whatever, whether of things that fly or walk or swim. Don't bow down to them and don't serve them because *I* am GOD, your God.

EXODUS 20:2-5

Hallelujah! It's a good thing to sing praise to our God; praise is beautiful, praise is fitting.

PSALM 147:1

I bless GOD every chance I get; my lungs expand with his praise.

PSALM 34:1

So here I am in the place of worship, eyes open, drinking in your strength and glory. In your generous love I am really living at last! My lips brim praises like fountains. I bless you every time I take a breath; my arms wave like banners of praise to you.

PSALM 63:2-4

REALITY CHECK

 Do you find yourself worshiping people or things? How does that experience compare to worshiping God?

○ How does praising God change you?

○ Is it possible to worship God even when you don't feel like it?

○ Why would God put so much emphasis on worship?

Prayer

Lord, I love You and can hardly believe that You love me even more. I thank You for giving me life, for establishing a purpose for me, for all the blessings You've granted me, and for sending Your Son to die for me. I do want to worship and serve You, not false gods or images or ideas. Help me to sing Your praises daily and to draw closer to You with every moment of worship. Praise be to the Lord of lords and King of kings! Amen.

PRAYER

How can I find God day by day?

Don't you hate it when one of your friends won't talk to you? You send e-mails, leave messages on the answering machine, and there's no response. Or you're actually in the same room, trying to have a conversation, and all you're getting back is, "Uh-huh. Fine. Whatever." It's tough to keep a friendship going when you're the only one trying to communicate.

It's the same for God. It's true that He already knows what you need and what you're thinking (see Matthew 6:8). But He wants more. He longs for direct communication—a *relationship* with you. That's why Paul said we should "Pray all the time" (1 Thessalonians 5:17). Prayer

Prayer
KNOWING GOD

is our link to heaven. It's our incredible opportunity to sit down anytime we want and "have a cup of coffee" with our Lord. He is always available and ready to spend time with you: "GOD's there, listening for all who pray, for all who pray and mean it" (Psalm 145:18). Of course, it's more for our benefit than His. As we pray daily, we find ourselves growing closer to God, to His will, and to a deeper understanding of what life is all about: "Call to me and I will answer you. I'll tell you marvelous and wondrous things that you could never figure out on your own" (Jeremiah 33:3).

Whether you're dealing with a friend, a potential boyfriend or girlfriend, or God, the rules are the same—getting to know someone on a close, intimate level requires opening up and talking on a regular basis. As a Christian leader once said, "God desires a relationship with each one of us, and there's no relationship in eavesdropping!"

GOD'S ADVICE

If you seek GOD, your God, you'll be able to find him if you're serious, looking for him with your whole heart and soul.

DEUTERONOMY 4:29

With all my might I shout up to GOD, his answers thunder from the holy mountain.

PSALM 3:4

Open up before GOD, keep nothing back; he'll do whatever needs to be done.

PSALM 37:5

"When two of you get together on anything at all on earth and make a prayer of it, my Father in heaven goes into action. And when two or three of you are together because of me, you can be sure that I'll be there."

MATTHEW 18:19-20

"Before they call out, I'll answer. Before they've finished speaking, I'll have heard."

ISAIAH 65:24

Every time I'm in trouble I call on you, confident that you'll answer.

PSALM 86:7

Prayer
KNOWING GOD

REALITY CHECK

○ How close are you to your friends? How close are you to God?

○ How often do you talk to God: Hourly? Daily? Weekly? Monthly?

○ How does God answer you—or does He?

○ When you talk to friends, do you usually keep the conversation on a safe, surface level, or do you like to "go deep"? What about when you talk to God?

Write and Reflect

For the next week, make it a point to pray to God at least three times a day. After each "conversation," write down what you prayed about. At the end of the week, take a look at your prayers and your relationship with God and see if anything is changing.

FAITH

My "believing" comes and goes.
What's the problem?

You probably remember them from high school — guys or girls who always followed the latest trends, whether it was movies, fashion, or who was popular that week. They were your very best friend, but only until someone new came along. They rarely studied. They made few commitments, and the ones they did they didn't keep. The term that best described them was *immature*.

Our faith can be like that too. Remember Peter when he joined Jesus in walking on the lake? At first all was fine, but then a gust of wind scared him and he began to sink, causing Jesus to ask, "Why did you doubt?" (see Matthew 14:29-31). Or Thomas, who said he wouldn't believe Jesus had returned until he saw Him with his own eyes (John 20:25).

If your faith comes and goes, that's okay. Many times the disciples' faith wavered as well. It only means that you have more growing to do to reach spiritual maturity. (Here's another tip—we all have room to grow spiritually!) Like Peter, we must keep our eyes always focused on Christ, not letting ourselves be distracted by matters of the world. Like Thomas, we should realize that faith is not a matter of seeing, but of trusting and believing in what we "don't yet see" (2 Corinthians 5:7). Spiritual maturity doesn't come with age. It comes with seeking and growing in Jesus day by day.

GOD'S ADVICE

The fundamental fact of existence is that this trust in God, this faith, is the firm foundation under everything that makes life worth living. It's our handle on what we can't see.

HEBREWS 11:1

We preach Christ, warning people not to add to the Message. We teach in a spirit of profound common sense so that we can bring each person to maturity. To be mature is to be basic. Christ! No more, no less.

COLOSSIANS 1:28

No prolonged infancies among us, please. We'll not tolerate babes in the woods, small children who are an easy mark for imposters. God wants us to grow up, to know the whole truth and tell it in love—like Christ in everything.

EPHESIANS 4:14-15

Run away from infantile indulgence. Run after mature righteousness—faith, love, peace—joining those who are in honest and serious prayer before God.

2 TIMOTHY 2:22

Now, like infants at the breast, drink deep of God's pure kindness. Then you'll grow up mature and whole in God.

1 PETER 2:2

Faith
KNOWING GOD

REALITY CHECK

○ Be honest—do you ever doubt your faith, or even that God exists?

○ Are you a person who relies on provable facts—the idea that "seeing is believing"?

○ On a scale of 1 to 10, how would you rate your level of spiritual maturity?

○ What steps are you taking to develop your faith? What more could you do?

○ What does Paul mean when he says to "run after mature righteousness" (2 Timothy 2:22)?

Prayer

Lord, I feel like the man who cried out to Jesus, "I believe. Help me with my doubts!" (Mark 9:24). I desire to put my whole trust in You, yet I struggle with doubt. Help me! Show me how to grow spiritually, to discover what it means to be a mature follower of You. Thank You for reminding me that even the disciples had times of shaky faith. Please allow my faith to grow a little each day. Amen.

GRACE

What if I keep screwing up?
Can God still use me?

What would you think of an impulsive guy with a nasty temper who never seemed to understand what you were trying to tell him? A guy you had to reprimand because he rejected your words to your face? A guy who, when you were in the worst jam of your life, pretended he didn't even know you? If you're like most people, you wouldn't have much use for this screwup. You certainly wouldn't see any future for him.

But Jesus isn't like most people. When He encountered a guy like that—a man named Simon, whom Jesus renamed Peter—He saw what others didn't. Jesus not only forgave Peter for his foolishness, but He embraced

Grace

him and entrusted him with the tasks of saving His people and building His church. The "screwup" became perhaps the most important human figure in the history of Christianity.

Sooner or later, you're going to blow it too. You're going to do something that offends God deeply and puts a big-time wedge into your relationship with Him. You're going to think that He won't want anything to do with you—and that He certainly can't use you anymore to glorify His kingdom. What's amazing, however, is that you'll be wrong. You can remove that wedge by sincerely asking for God's forgiveness. He isn't keeping a list of your sins (Isaiah 43:25). And then, by His grace, He'll allow the "new" you to serve Him in an incredible way that you never expected—just like Peter.

GOD'S ADVICE

If we admit our sins—make a clean breast of them—he won't let us down; he'll be true to himself. He'll forgive our sins and purge us of all wrongdoing.

1 JOHN 1:9

Let's walk right up to him and get what he is so ready to give. Take the mercy, accept the help.

HEBREWS 4:16

Every detail works to your advantage and to God's glory: more and more grace, more and more people, more and more praise!

2 CORINTHIANS 4:15

I write this, dear children, to guide you out of sin. But if anyone does sin, we have a Priest-Friend in the presence of the Father: Jesus Christ, righteous Jesus.

1 JOHN 2:1

Anyone united with the Messiah gets a fresh start, is created new. The old life is gone; a new life burgeons!

2 CORINTHIANS 5:17

Grace
KNOWING GOD

REALITY CHECK

◯ What's the biggest mistake you ever made? Where do you stand with God on that?

◯ Do you believe that God doesn't hold things against you?

◯ Have you met people, like Peter, who seem to have trouble "getting it right"? How do you respond to people like this?

◯ What is your definition of grace?

Write and Reflect

In the space below, write about times that you've messed up, and about how God has used you in new ways afterward.

FRIENDSHIP

How can I have a personal relationship with a God I can't see or hear?

Now that high school's over and done with, you and many of your friends are probably moving on to different cities and regions, even different countries. It's going to be a challenge keeping up long distance with those friends, but you know you can do it through e-mail, phone calls, cards, and letters. Though they're no longer physically present, your relationships with them can continue to grow and thrive. Those friends will still have a tremendous influence on your life.

It's true that we can't physically *see* God—but it's certainly just as true that He is with us, loving and influencing us, desiring a relationship that grows ever deeper over time. He speaks to us through the words of His Message. He guides us when He answers prayers by opening or closing the door on opportunities. He encourages us through the words and actions of others. He's closer to us than any of those friends who moved away: "God himself is right alongside to keep you steady and on track until things are all wrapped up by Jesus" (1 Corinthians 1:8).

Just as with your friends, however, you can't expect your relationship with God to grow by itself. You have to "water" it—not with e-mails, phone calls, and letters but with prayers, worship, and times of reflection on His Message. Stay focused on those things and you'll find God overcoming any distance to be right there with you.

GOD'S ADVICE

Say a quiet *yes* to God and he'll be there in no time.

JAMES 4:8

We saw it, we heard it, and now we're telling you so you can experience it along with us, this experience of communion with the Father and his Son, Jesus Christ.

1 JOHN 1:3

"I'll stay with you, I'll protect you wherever you go."

GENESIS 28:15

"You are my friends when you do the things I command you. I'm no longer calling you servants because servants don't understand what their master is thinking and planning. No, I've named you friends because I've let you in on everything I've heard from the Father."

JOHN 15:14-15

"Look at me. I stand at the door. I knock. If you hear me call and open the door, I'll come right in and sit down to supper with you."

REVELATION 3:20

REALITY CHECK

○ Do you have a hard time keeping up with faraway friends? Why?

○ What's most important to you in a friendship—conversation? Someone to do things with? Similar likes and dislikes?

○ What's most important to you in your relationship with God?

○ Have you ever felt God "telling" you something? What was it?

Write and Reflect

Make a list of times when your relationship with God was strong and you felt His presence. What was going on in your life then? Write down some of the reasons why God seemed close.

JOY

Is happiness real?

On a day when you earn a D- on your midterm exam, lose your job at the convenience store, and get dumped by your boyfriend, *happiness* can sound like a foreign concept. Dictionaries define *happy* as "feeling or showing pleasure, contentment, or joy." It's tough to sense anything like that when your life is falling apart. Even when things are okay, you may still wonder if genuine happiness—the kind that never goes away—truly exists.

The apostle Paul had something to say about that. He once described a group of Macedonian believers this way: "Fierce troubles came down on the people of those churches, pushing them to the very limit. The trial exposed their true colors: They were incredibly happy, though desperately poor. The pressure triggered something totally unexpected: an outpouring of pure and generous gifts. . . . They gave offerings of whatever they could—far more than they could afford!—pleading for the privilege of helping out in the relief of poor Christians (2 Corinthians 8:2-4).

Fierce troubles . . . desperately poor . . . incredibly happy. *How*, you ask, *do those fit together?* The answer is God. When we have a loving and growing relationship with our heavenly Father, we *can* know real contentment and happiness because real happiness *is* joy. The more we delight in God's presence, the less we're influenced by temporary emotions or circumstances. If we're believers, a turn for the worse can even remind us how much we *do* have and what we can offer to others. The source of real happiness can only be found in heaven.

GOD'S ADVICE

I'm just as happy with little as with much, with much as with little. I've found the recipe for being happy whether full or hungry, hands full or hands empty. Whatever I have, wherever I am, I can make it through anything in the One who makes me who I am.

PHILIPPIANS 4:12-13

Count yourself lucky, how happy you must be—you get a fresh start, your slate's wiped clean.

PSALM 32:1

Stalwart walks in step with GOD; his path blazed by GOD, he's happy. If he stumbles, he's not down for long; GOD has a grip on his hand.

PSALM 37:23-24

I inherited your book on living; it's mine forever—what a gift! And how happy it makes me!

PSALM 119:111

You made me so happy, GOD. I saw your work and I shouted for joy.

PSALM 92:4

Joy

REALITY CHECK

○ When was the last time you felt truly happy? What prompted that feeling?

○ Do you know people who are always joyful, regardless of what's happening? What's their secret?

○ Have you ever felt happy or content when life was a disaster?

○ Do troubles usually move you closer to God or further away?

Prayer

Dear God, I am so thankful for Your presence in my life! Please forgive me for the times when I let bad days interrupt the joy You offer. Help me, like Paul, to be happy in You "whether full or hungry, hands full or hands empty." Show me how, like the Macedonians, to turn my own problems into opportunities for greater happiness and glory for You. Amen.

BECOMING ME

OBEDIENCE

Is there a difference between following my passions and following God?

From the time that he was a little boy, Jim knew that he wanted to be an artist. He had a passion for drawing and painting and a talent to match. During high school, however, he sensed God urging him to give up his ambition and turn instead to a life of ministry. He didn't listen. After high school, Jim enrolled in an art institute and graduated at the top of his class. He had exciting plans for the future, and nothing was going to stop him.

Except that things didn't work out the way Jim expected. Despite his talent, he couldn't find a job in the art world. He eventually turned to pumping gas at a service station—a humbling experience for a great artist!

It was seven long years after his high school graduation that Jim finally gave in, opened up his heart to God, and let go of his dream of becoming an artist. He went into the ministry and served for decades as a successful pastor, never regretting his new life. He also discovered that his artistic talent wasn't wasted. Jim continued to draw and paint, using those skills to further his ministry.[1]

God's position is clear: He loves us, He knows what's best for us, and He demands our obedience. His ideas for who we are and what we can become are always bigger and better than ours. Your plans and passions *may* be part of God's will for you—but to know for sure, see if they fall in line with the teaching of His Message, then ask Him directly through prayer.

GOD'S ADVICE

We plan the way we want to live, but only GOD makes us able to live it.

PROVERBS 16:9

Trust GOD from the bottom of your heart; don't try to figure out everything on your own. Listen for GOD's voice in everything you do, everywhere you go; he's the one who will keep you on track.

PROVERBS 3:5-6

And now I have a word for you who brashly announce, "Today—at the latest, tomorrow—we're off to such and such a city for the year. We're going to start a business and make a lot of money." You don't know the first thing about tomorrow. You're nothing but a wisp of fog, catching a brief bit of sun before disappearing. Instead, make it a habit to say, "If the Master wills it and we're still alive, we'll do this or that." As it is, you are full of your grandiose selves. All such vaunting self-importance is evil.

JAMES 4:13-16

"Obey me. Do what I say and I will be your God and you will be my people. Live the way I tell you. Do what I command so that your lives will go well."

JEREMIAH 7:23

"Call to me and I will answer you. I'll tell you marvelous and wondrous things that you could never figure out on your own."

JEREMIAH 33:3

Obedience

BECOMING ME

REALITY CHECK

○ What are you truly passionate about?

○ Where do you sense that God stands on those passions? How do you know?

○ How do you typically respond to the authority figures in your life: teachers? parents? God?

○ How often do you compare your passions to God's Word? How often do you run them by Him in prayer?

○ How do you respond to this statement: "God created me, so these passions inside me must be from Him"?

Prayer

Dear God, I'm so glad that You know everything, and that You love me to the point of having a perfect plan for me. Please share Your wisdom with me. Help me to know where to go. You know all that I want and hope for. Help me to focus my efforts toward Your goals, with Your passion. Enable my ambition to be motivated by love for You and for others (Matthew 22:34-40). Though I can't always see Your vision for the future, I'm thankful that You always have my best in mind. Amen.

COURAGE

How can I face the world when I'm scared to even get out of bed?

It's exciting to be on your own for the first time and calling all the shots (will it be pizza or Chinese food tonight?). It can also be scary. You may be dealing with all kinds of issues—moving, enrolling in college, starting a full-time job, managing a budget, choosing an apartment or roommate, buying a car. You may be intimidated by a professor or a new boss. And then there are relationships, which may also be getting more intense. High school was hard enough! Now you're up against greater expectations, increased responsibilities, and choices that will influence the rest of your life. The pressure can make it seem like each new day is a disaster waiting to

Courage

BECOMING ME

52

happen—so why get out of bed at all?

The apostle Paul knew something about pressure and fear. When he first approached the Corinthians to tell them about Christ, he felt "unsure," "inadequate," and "scared to death." In his words, "nothing I said could have impressed you or anyone else." So Paul did the one sensible thing he knew to do—he trusted God to help him. Paul's message was successfully delivered; "God's Spirit and God's power did it."

God is always at your side; He's with you "every step you take" (Joshua 1:9). If you continue to love Him, seek Him, and trust Him, you'll discover He's giving you the daily courage you need to get through even the scariest moments.

GOD'S ADVICE

"No weapon that can hurt you has ever been forged. . . . This is what GOD's servants can expect. I'll see to it that everything works out for the best."

ISAIAH 54:17

Even when the way goes through Death Valley, I'm not afraid when you walk at my side.

PSALM 23:4

There is no room in love for fear. Well-formed love banishes fear. Since fear is crippling, a fearful life—fear of death, fear of judgment—is one not yet fully formed in love.

1 JOHN 4:18

No need to panic over alarms or surprises,
or predictions that doomsday's just around the corner,
Because GOD will be right there with you;
he'll keep you safe and sound.

PROVERBS 3:25-26

Courage

BECOMING ME

REALITY CHECK

○ What scares you the most about this next week? The next year? The rest of your life?

○ How do you usually handle mind-numbing fear: Confront it? Avoid it? Talk about it? Pray about it?

○ Can you see a godly purpose for fear?

○ Do you agree with John's statement that a fearful life "is one not yet fully formed in love" (1 John 4:18)?

○ How exactly does God provide courage?

Prayer

Father, I want to love and trust You, but sometimes I feel so overwhelmed and afraid that I can't seem to go on. Thank You for understanding me, for promising to stand by me no matter what, and for giving me the courage I need to face enemies and obstacles with confidence. Help me to remember that You and Your love are bigger than any problem I'll ever face. Amen.

FORGIVENESS | *How can I forgive?*

You know what you're supposed to do. It's there in black and white: "Forgive one another as quickly and thoroughly as God in Christ forgave you" (Ephesians 4:32). But how can God possibly expect you to forgive *this*?

Whatever your friend's discretion—she lied about you, stole from you, revealed your deepest secret, went out with your boyfriend—God *does* expect you to forgive her. You won't be able to do it on your own, but if you ask for His grace and strength you can approach your friend, gently point out her wrong, and offer genuine forgiveness—"seventy times seven" times if necessary (Matthew 18:22).

Forgiveness

It's not just for the sake of your friend. God knows what will happen to you if you don't forgive — bitterness will begin to fester and grow inside you like a weed on steroids. Worse, it will separate you from your Master: "If you refuse to do your part, you cut yourself off from God's part" (Matthew 6:15). *Not fair!* you say. Maybe not. But ask yourself this: Was it "fair" for Jesus to suffer and die for our mistakes? Even as He was dying, He prayed, "Father, forgive them; they don't know what they're doing" (Luke 23:34). He knows it isn't easy, yet He has set the example. Our job is to rely on Him as we follow it.

GOD'S ADVICE

"Be alert. If you see your friend going wrong, correct him. If he responds, forgive him. Even if it's personal against you and repeated seven times through the day, and seven times he says, 'I'm sorry, I won't do it again,' forgive him."

"Listen to this carefully. I'm warning you. There's nothing done or said that can't be forgiven."

MARK 3:28

At that point Peter got up the nerve to ask, "Master, how many times do I forgive a brother or sister who hurts me? Seven?" Jesus replied, "Seven! Hardly. Try seventy times seven."

MATTHEW 18:21-22

"And when you assume the posture of prayer, remember that it's not all asking. If you have anything against someone, forgive—only then will your heavenly Father be inclined to also wipe your slate clean of sins."

MARK 11:25

"If you forgive someone's sins, they're gone for good. If you don't forgive sins, what are you going to do with them?"

JOHN 20:23

Forgiveness

BECOMING ME

REALITY CHECK

○ What's the worst thing anyone ever did to you? Were you able to forgive that person? *Broken my heart. No, not truly.*

○ What's the worst thing you ever did to someone? Were you forgiven?

○ What happens to you when you don't forgive, or don't forgive quickly? *The guilt builds until its all I think about.*

○ When it comes to forgiveness, do you think God is asking too much? *No, if he could give his son to die to forgive us, we can forgive others.*

The Next Step

Make a list of the specific times when people have hurt you the most in your life. Cross off the ones you've already gone to and forgiven. Now pray about the rest of your list! If you sense God's leading, make a plan for approaching these people and gently—and genuinely—choosing to forgive them.

Adrienne- not telling a/bme & TC.
Cody - forgiving him for hating him / breaking my heart.

SERVICE

No doubt you've heard of what some Christians call "The Great Commission," the charge given by the risen Jesus to the disciples: "Go out and train everyone you meet, far and near, in this way of life, marking them by baptism in the threefold name: Father, Son, and Holy Spirit. Then instruct them in the practice of all I have commanded you" (Matthew 28:19-20).

For some, that means going to the far reaches of the globe to deliver Christ's message. At age twenty, for instance, Melissa has already completed mission trips to Mexico and East Timor, and she is currently reaching out to prostitutes in Australia by offering food and friendship along with God's Word. Answering the Lord's call, however, doesn't always require such dramatic or far-flung ministry. It can start right where you live and be as simple as listening respectfully when your roommate has a complaint, refusing to shortchange your employer even when everyone else is doing it, or lending a hand to the neighbor who's just moving in. The "little" things you do now can eventually lead to big opportunities to introduce someone to God.

Look again at the words of Jesus: "Go out and train everyone you meet, *far and near* . . ." (emphasis added). If God is telling you to go to Africa and help solve the AIDS crisis as you spread His Word, great! If not, it may be that His purpose for you is at your apartment complex, at your work, or with an old friend. Pray for guidance and let Him show you the way.

GOD'S ADVICE

Don't let anyone put you down because you're young. Teach believers with your life: by word, by demeanor, by love, by faith, by integrity.

1 TIMOTHY 4:12

Show them all this by doing it yourself, incorruptible in your teaching, your words solid and sane. Then anyone who is dead set against us, when he finds nothing weird or misguided, might eventually come around.

TITUS 2:7-8

Do your best. Work from the heart for your real Master, for God, confident that you'll get paid in full when you come into your inheritance. Keep in mind always that the ultimate Master you're serving is Christ.

COLOSSIANS 3:22-24

"This is how everyone will recognize that you are my disciples—when they see the love you have for each other."

JOHN 13:35

REALITY CHECK

○ Do you sense God calling you to serve Him in a place other than where you are?

○ What are your current opportunities to serve?

○ Paul told Timothy to "teach believers with your life" (1 Timothy 4:12). Are you doing that? How?

○ How has the example of other believers encouraged you in the past?

○ Do you feel competent or inadequate as a "spokesman" for God? Why?

Write and Reflect

Make a list of possible ways to serve God in the next week. Choose at least three of them and come up with a detailed plan to make them happen. At the end of the week, ask God what your next step should be.

SERENITY

I worry all the time. Can I stop these voices in my head?

Do you ever hear voices? Not the ones of your neighbors arguing in the dorm room next door, but nagging voices inside your head, constantly questioning you and your future? *Where will I get the money to pay rent next month? I hate my major — will I ever find a career I like? My girlfriend's been distant lately — is she seeing someone else?* Those voices certainly aren't from God.

The years after high school are among the most stressful of your life. With everything changing, from living spaces to relationships to career choices to the quality of food you eat ("Mom, I miss your cooking!"), a certain amount of fear and anxiety is natural. What isn't part of the nature of believers who rely on God, however, is a feeling of inner turmoil that never goes away.

God has a different idea for your life. He will take care of you if you trust Him. He wants you to focus on Him and be at peace no matter what your circumstances: "Give your entire attention to what God is doing right now, and don't get worked up about what may or may not happen tomorrow. God will help you deal with whatever hard things come up when the time comes" (Matthew 6:34). When the voices in your head are competing for attention, listen to the one that counts—and tune out the rest.

GOD'S ADVICE

Don't fret or worry. Instead of worrying, pray. Let petitions and praises shape your worries into prayers, letting God know your concerns. Before you know it, a sense of God's wholeness, everything coming together for good, will come and settle you down. It's wonderful what happens when Christ displaces worry at the center of your life.

PHILIPPIANS 4:6-7

"I'm leaving you well and whole. That's my parting gift to you. Peace. I don't leave you the way you're used to being left—feeling abandoned, bereft. So don't be upset. Don't be distraught."

JOHN 14:27

So be content with who you are, and don't put on airs. God's strong hand is on you; he'll promote you at the right time. Live carefree before God; he is most careful with you.

1 PETER 5:6-7

Let the peace of Christ keep you in tune with each other.

COLOSSIANS 3:15

My grace is enough; it's all you need. My strength comes into its own in your weakness.

2 CORINTHIANS 12:9

Serenity

BECOMING ME

REALITY CHECK

○ Do worries often overwhelm you?

○ What are your biggest concerns right now? How are you dealing with them?

○ What does Peter mean by "Live carefree before God" (1 Peter 5:7)?

○ Are some problems just too big to let go of? Do you think God expects you to put them out of your mind?

○ When in your life have you most felt at peace?

The Next Step

Read Matthew 6:25-34 *every day* for the next week. Pray about it. Let God in on any concerns you have. Then watch and listen for His response.

ATTITUDE

My life stinks. How do I become genuinely thankful?

"Thank God no matter what happens." That's what Paul wrote to the Thessalonians (1 Thessalonians 5:18). It sounds good, but surely it doesn't apply when you're broke, you're flunking your major at school, and your mom is dying of cancer. Who can be thankful at a time like that, right?

When your life is a disaster, God doesn't ask you to pretend that you're not struggling, scared, and hurting. But He *does* ask you to be thankful. Why? Because He is there to lead you through even the worst nightmare. Because He can use your bad situations to teach you and others more about Him. Because every misfortune is an opportunity to dive deeper into His love. Because He knows how it all turns out — and when you're a believer, that means a happy ending, regardless of the twists and turns along the way.

Remember, Paul gave up a life of power and prestige to follow Jesus. He spent years in prison because of His ministry. He was afflicted with health problems. He was martyred. Yet He found himself "glad in God, far happier than you would ever guess" (Philippians 4:10). An "attitude of gratitude" isn't based on whether you're having a good week or a bad week. It's based on knowing how the story ends — and loving a God who loves you more than you can imagine.

GOD'S ADVICE

Be cheerful no matter what; pray all the time; thank God no matter what happens. This is the way God wants you who belong to Christ Jesus to live.

1 THESSALONIANS 5:16-18

Cultivate thankfulness. Let the Word of Christ—the Message—have the run of the house.

COLOSSIANS 3:15-16

Sing songs from your heart to Christ. Sing praises over everything, any excuse for a song to God the Father in the name of our Master, Jesus Christ.

EPHESIANS 5:19-20

Give thanks to GOD—he is good and his love never quits.

1 CHRONICLES 16:34

Do you see what we've got? An unshakable kingdom! And do you see how thankful we must be? Not only thankful, but brimming with worship, deeply reverent before God.

HEBREWS 12:28

Attitude

BECOMING ME

REALITY CHECK

○ How do you show thankfulness to others? To God?

○ What are you most thankful for right now?

○ What is most difficult for you to be thankful for right now?

○ Do you sometimes say you're thankful for things without meaning it?

○ Whom do you know who displays an attitude of gratitude? What's his or her secret?

Prayer

Dear God, I want to say "Thank You" for so many things—for Your love, for Your patience with my ungratefulness, for Your presence in my life, for Your guidance, for the hope You provide no matter how bad my life gets. I know I can never repay You for what You've done and continue to do for me. Most of all, I thank You for Jesus and for the incredible future I know You're planning for me. I can't wait! Amen.

OWNING MY FAITH

CHURCH

I'd rather deal with God on my own.
I don't need church — do I?

To a lot of people, "church" means a building with pews and pulpits and burning candles. Do you need all that? No, not really. But the church you *do* need is the one defined by God: membership in the body of Christ (see 1 Corinthians 12:12-27). The idea here is to cultivate a continuous relationship with Christ and with fellow believers. It's essential to success as a Christian.

I agree with the Christ part, you say. *But I'm an independent operator. A free agent. A self-made man (or woman). I do better without anyone else in the equation.* If that's your line, you've bought into the culture's credo — the idea that we don't need anyone else, that, as one successful ad slogan put it, it's best to "fend for yourself." It's a false premise. As the apostle Paul said, "Can you imagine Eye telling Hand, 'Get lost; I don't need you'?" (1 Corinthians 12:21). "The way God designed our bodies is a model for understanding our lives together as a church: every part dependent on every other part" (1 Corinthians 12:25). It's true—we need each other if we're to achieve the kind of life and spiritual maturity that God has in mind.

In these first months and years after high school, as your days fill up with college classes, full-time work, or new relationships (or all of the above), it will be easy for you to let church slide. Don't. Find a group of believers that meets regularly for worship, prayer, Bible study, mutual encouragement and accountability, and outreach. It might be in a traditional church; it might not. What's important is that you stay connected to the body—no matter what your part.

GOD'S ADVICE

You are Christ's body — that's who you are! You must never forget this. Only as you accept your part of that body does your "part" mean anything.

1 CORINTHIANS 12:27

Let the peace of Christ keep you in tune with each other, in step with each other. None of this going off and doing your own thing.

COLOSSIANS 3:15

Let's see how inventive we can be in encouraging love and helping out, not avoiding worshiping together as some do but spurring each other on, especially as we see the big Day approaching.

HEBREWS 10:24-25

No one abuses his own body, does he? No, he feeds and pampers it. That's how Christ treats us, the church, since we are part of his body.

EPHESIANS 5:29-30

REALITY CHECK

○ What sounds more appealing—the idea of being spiritually dependent on others or the idea of being a spiritual "Lone Ranger"? Why?

○ What do you see as your part in the body of Christ?

○ What struggles, if any, do you encounter when you gather and worship with others?

○ When have church or fellowship groups led you closer to God?

Write and Reflect

In the space below, describe what "church" means to you—as well as any new thoughts that may have surfaced after today's reading.

RELATIONSHIPS

Does it really matter if I have sex with someone?

You're heavy into a relationship with a boyfriend or girl-friend and your thoughts are turning more and more to the sex thing—no surprise there! You've been taught (almost from the day you were born, it seems like) that there are certain things you can and cannot do with the opposite sex. For the most part, that makes sense. Yet you still find yourself wondering . . . will it *really* matter if you have sex with someone?

Let's answer that question with another: Who are the people that care most about your life? We'll leave out your boyfriend or girlfriend for now. Your parents, broth-ers, and sisters will certainly be on the list. Best friends will be there. People you especially respect, maybe a current professor or previous teacher in high school. Jesus, of course, should be at the top of the chart. And what about your future spouse? He or she will most definitely be on the list. So what will all of these folks say about what really matters?

Now let's ask someone else who should be high on your list—yourself. How important are *you* to you? Do you value yourself and your sexuality enough to save it for the person you'll spend your life with? Before you answer, consider the words of King David, speaking for all of God's creations: "Body and soul, I am marvelously made!" (Psalm 139:14). You were made in God's image. Your Father has loved you from even before you were born. It's safe to say that you and what you do matters to Him.

So does it matter if you have sex with someone? What do you think?

GOD'S ADVICE

With your very own hands you formed me; now breathe your wisdom over me so I can understand you.

PSALM 119:73

"What's the price of a pet canary? Some loose change, right? And God cares what happens to it even more than you do. He pays even greater attention to you, down to the last detail. . . . You're worth more than a million canaries."

MATTHEW 10:29-31

In sexual sin we violate the sacredness of our own bodies, these bodies that were made for God-given and God-modeled love, for "becoming one" with another. Or didn't you realize that your body is a sacred place, the place of the Holy Spirit? Don't you see that you can't live however you please, squandering what God paid such a high price for?

1 CORINTHIANS 6:18-19

Honor marriage, and guard the sacredness of sexual intimacy between wife and husband.

HEBREWS 13:4

Relationships

OWNING MY FAITH

REALITY CHECK

 Everyone talks about the importance of self-esteem—how does yours rate?

 What do you base your self-esteem (or lack of) on?

 In terms of your sex life, what attitude best shows love and respect for your boyfriend or girlfriend? What best shows love and respect for that person's future mate—whether it's you or someone else?

 In what way is your body a "sacred place" (1 Corinthians 6:19)?

Prayer

Father, I pray that You will open my eyes to my value in this world. Help me to see myself not through my own or others' distorted lenses, but as You see me—one of Your beloved children. Give me the strength to honor Your commands in the area of sexual intimacy and everywhere else. Amen.

KNOWLEDGE

Just what is truth, anyway?

You may have heard this one: A man, blind from birth, comes across a man named Jesus. This Jesus uses His own saliva to make a clay paste, rubs it on the blind man's eyes, and tells him to wash it off in a nearby pool. When the man does, he sees for the first time in his life. The local leaders grill him about what happened. Most are incensed that this healing was performed on a holy day, while a few wonder if the man named Jesus is a representative of God. In an uproar, they finally throw the once-blind man out. But the man, when he meets Jesus a second time, has no doubt. He worships Jesus (John 9).

What does this story have to do with truth? The

Pharisees were confounded by the account of the blind man. They couldn't fathom that a man of God, let alone a Savior, could or would perform healings on the Sabbath. It didn't fit with their previously established definition of truth, so they rejected the evidence altogether. The man, on the other hand, trusted his new experience. Though it didn't make sense according to anything he'd known before, he accepted the "impossible" and expanded his definition of truth.

Any "truth," whether it's based on reasoning about the past or experience of the present, depends on faith. You have faith that a chair you've never seen before will hold you up. The Pharisees had faith in their rules. And the blind man discovered life-changing faith in a personal encounter with Jesus. Christ said, "I came into the world to bring everything into the clear light of day, making all the distinctions clear, so that those who have never seen will see" (John 9:39). He *is* truth. You can have faith in that.

GOD'S ADVICE

"Anyone who examines this evidence will come to stake his life on this: that God himself is the truth."

JOHN 3:33

Avoid the talk-show religion and the practiced confusion of the so-called experts. People caught up in a lot of talk can miss the whole point of faith.

1 TIMOTHY 6:20-21

Where can you find someone truly wise, truly educated, truly intelligent in this day and age? Hasn't God exposed it all as pretentious nonsense? Since the world in all its fancy wisdom never had a clue when it came to knowing God, God in his wisdom took delight in using what the world considered dumb — *preaching*, of all things! — to bring those who trust him into the way of salvation.

1 CORINTHIANS 1:20-21

All they have eyes for is the fashionable god of darkness. They think he can give them what they want, and that they won't have to bother believing a Truth they can't see. They're stone-blind to the dayspring brightness of the Message that shines with Christ, who gives us the best picture of God we'll ever get.

2 CORINTHIANS 4:4

"Then you will experience for yourselves the truth, and the truth will free you."

JOHN 8:32

Knowledge

OWNING MY FAITH

REALITY CHECK

○ What's your definition of *truth?*

○ How does faith influence not only what you believe about God, but everything you see as true in your world?

○ How would you communicate truth to your friends?

○ What is an effective way to share what you believe?

○ What does it mean that "God himself is the truth" (John 3:33)?

Write and Reflect

Make a list of ten nonnegotiable truths about God. Think about why you believe in these spiritual truths and what these truths mean for your life.

ANGER

If Jesus can turn over tables in church, is it wrong for me to be angry?

You know the story—it's right there in the second chapter of John. Jesus was so mad at the people selling animals and exchanging money in the temple that He made a whip and chased them out, yelling "Get your things out of here! Stop turning my Father's house into a shopping mall!" (John 2:16). If Jesus could show that kind of anger, we can too, right?

Well, not so fast. There's a difference between the righteous anger Jesus displayed in the temple and the anger you may feel when someone cuts in front of you in line or steals your new DVD player. Of course you're going to be mad when something like that happens.

Those feelings are natural. But how you deal with them is a different matter. Jesus is God—He had the authority to drive offenders out of His church. You don't.

So what *are* you supposed to do with your anger? Look for the answer in Ephesians 4:26: "You do well to be angry—but don't use your anger as fuel for revenge." In other words, it's okay to be mad, and it's okay to let that guy know you're unhappy and want your DVD player returned. What *isn't* okay is getting back at him by punching him in the face, slashing his tires, and stealing his entire stereo system. God says that revenge belongs to Him (Romans 12:19). If you get angry, it's best to let go of it quickly to keep evil at a distance (Ephesians 4:27) and instead deal with the situation with "deep understanding" (Proverbs 14:29). That's not always easy, but Jesus will be there to help you through it. He understands how you feel.

GOD'S ADVICE

Go ahead and be angry. You do well to be angry—but don't use your anger as fuel for revenge. And don't stay angry. Don't go to bed angry. Don't give the Devil that kind of foothold in your life.

EPHESIANS 4:26-27

Lead with your ears, follow up with your tongue, and let anger straggle along in the rear. God's righteousness doesn't grow from human anger.

JAMES 1:19-20

A gentle response defuses anger, but a sharp tongue kindles a temper-fire.

PROVERBS 15:1

"Count yourselves blessed every time people put you down or throw you out or speak lies about you to discredit me. . . . You can be glad when that happens—give a cheer, even!—for though they don't like it, *I* do!"

MATTHEW 5:11-12

Slowness to anger makes for deep understanding; a quick-tempered person stockpiles stupidity.

PROVERBS 14:29

Don't insist on getting even; that's not for you to do. "I'll do the judging," says God. "I'll take care of it."

ROMANS 12:19

Anger

OWNING MY FAITH

REALITY CHECK

○ Are you usually slow to anger or more quick-tempered?

○ When was the last time you got really angry? Was it a righteous anger or motivated more by a desire for revenge?

○ What helps you let go of anger? What happens when you don't let go?

○ Do you trust God enough to let Him "do the judging" (Romans 12:19) when you've been wronged?

Prayer

Dear God, I know I have a temper. When someone hurts me or takes advantage of me I seem to overflow with rage! Yet I know that I want to let Jesus shine through me in the ways that I handle difficult situations. Show me how to be slow to anger, and when I do get mad, help me to get rid of it in a manner that is pleasing and brings glory to You. Amen.

TEMPTATION

I know I shouldn't . . . but what if I really want to?

You've had a great evening together. Now it's just you and her, alone, sitting on the couch in your apartment. She's always been attractive, but tonight she's—well, the only word that fits is "hot." When you put your arm around her, she snuggles up closer. This is definitely getting interesting. And then . . .

Okay, hold up. . . . You might want to consider where the evening is going to end up if you continue. You've just entered the "danger zone" of temptation described by Jesus (Mark 14:38). When your body heat rises, your heart starts pounding, and your breathing rate doubles, you're not in a position to make reasonable choices. You

Temptation

know you shouldn't keep going, but you're beyond caring. Which means you're headed for trouble!

Temptation—whether it's sexual, ethical, spiritual, or any other kind—is part of life. Even Jesus faced temptation while in the wilderness (see Matthew 4:1-11). What's important is how you respond to it. If you find yourself wavering on what seemed a clear-cut position at the beginning of the day, that's a definite sign that you're in the danger zone. Jesus countered temptation by repeatedly quoting Scripture, an example for all of us to follow. Another great defense is found in the third chapter of Proverbs: "Run to GOD! Run from evil!" (verse 7). Temptation can't take hold of you if it can't find you.

Here's a smart strategy: Decide where you stand on issues that might tempt you *before* they come up. Then when you do face temptation, hold your ground—or run as fast as you can in the opposite direction.

GOD'S ADVICE

Keep your eyes straight ahead; ignore all sideshow distractions. Watch your step, and the road will stretch out smooth before you. Look neither right nor left; leave evil in the dust.

PROVERBS 4:25-27

"Stay alert, be in prayer, so you don't enter the danger zone without even knowing it."

MARK 14:38

We don't have a priest who is out of touch with our reality. He's been through weakness and testing, experienced it all—all but the sin. So let's walk right up to him and get what he is so ready to give. Take the mercy, accept the help.

HEBREWS 4:15-16

How can a young person live a clean life? By carefully reading the map of your Word.

PSALM 119:9

No test or temptation that comes your way is beyond the course of what others have had to face. All you need to remember is that God will never let you down; he'll never let you be pushed past your limit; he'll always be there to help you come through it.

1 CORINTHIANS 10:13

Yell a loud *no* to the Devil and watch him scamper. Say a quiet *yes* to God and he'll be there in no time.

JAMES 4:7-8

Temptation

OWNING MY FAITH

REALITY CHECK

○ When has temptation gotten the better of you in the past?
Going further (sexually) than I planned.

○ When has God helped you achieve victory over temptation? *Talking w/ my partner and reaching an agreement.*

○ In what areas of your life do you most struggle with temptation? ~~██~~ *thoughts of a future that hasn't happened yet.*

○ What could you do to minimize the danger in these areas? *Fill my mind w/ positive thoughts.*

○ What Scripture is most encouraging to you in dealing with temptation? *James 4:7-8*

Write and Reflect

Read 1 Corinthians 10:1-13. Now make a list of a few times that you gave in to temptation. Beside each entry on the list, write down ways that God may have provided an escape from that temptation if you'd been looking for it.

MONEY

What happens when I have faith, but no cash?

When it comes to finances, those first years after high school can be rough. Expenses such as college loans, buying and maintaining a car, and paying rent for the first time can leave you searching through pockets and under cushions for every spare nickel. Without a spending plan, your financial situation can go from disappointing to disastrous faster than you can say "put it on my credit card."

God wants you to be a good steward of the resources He gives you, and that includes your money. Tithing—the practice of giving at least 10 percent of your income back to God—is more important than ever when your cash flow has dried up. It's your giving that puts you in the best position to be blessed by Him. Remember, it was the woman who gave just two coins—all that she had—who earned the highest praise from Jesus (see Mark 12:41-44).

There's more to being a good steward of your money. You might start with this simple rule: If you don't have it, don't spend it. Credit card companies specifically target high school graduates because they hope to get you hooked on the habit of spending beyond your means. Another good idea is to set aside as much money as you can. When your savings start piling up instead of your debts, you're on the right track. On the subject of money, however, the most important rule to remember is to place your trust not in wealth, but in God.

GOD'S ADVICE

A devout life does bring wealth, but it's the rich simplicity of being yourself before God. Since we entered the world penniless and will leave it penniless, if we have bread on the table and shoes on our feet, that's enough.

1 TIMOTHY 6:6-8

Tell those rich in this world's wealth to quit being so full of themselves and so obsessed with money, which is here today and gone tomorrow. Tell them to go after God, who piles on all the riches we could ever manage — to do good, to be rich in helping others, to be extravagantly generous. If they do that, they'll build a treasury that will last, gaining life that is truly life.

1 TIMOTHY 6:17-19

"Bring your full tithe to the Temple treasury so there will be ample provisions in my Temple. Test me in this and see if I don't open up heaven itself to you and pour out blessings beyond your wildest dreams."

MALACHI 3:10

Don't be obsessed with getting more material things. Be relaxed with what you have.

HEBREWS 13:5

"Are you penniless? Come anyway — buy and eat!
Come, buy your drinks, buy wine and milk. Buy without money — everything's free!"

ISAIAH 55:1

Money

OWNING MY FAITH

REALITY CHECK

○ How important is money to you? What annual salary would you consider "enough"?

○ Do you live on a budget?

○ Do you bring glory to God in the way you handle your money?

○ Does it feel spiritual or selfish to give so that you can be blessed by God?

○ What are the biggest advantages to having money? What are the biggest disadvantages?

The Next Step

If you aren't already doing this, try making a record of *everything* you spend for the next two weeks. Divide your expenses into categories—God, groceries, school, entertainment, and so on. At the end of the two weeks, evaluate where your money is going. Are you surprised by anything you see? Are any changes in order? If it seems appropriate, use your figures to establish a budget—then stick to it.

MARRIAGE

I've found "the one" . . . I think. How can I know for sure?

You've done it! You've found "the one." He or she is everything you've been looking for: attractive, intelligent, charming, and sweet. Great sense of humor. Definite heart for God. Best of all, you're both madly in love. You've never felt anything like this before!

Yet you want to be sure. It's hard to imagine problems now, but how can you know that "the one" today won't make you want to run tomorrow? You might start by looking again at that little word called *love*. From God's point of view, love has a lot less to do with how your partner makes *you* feel and everything to do with how much you want to give to your partner. Is yours a love that "never gives up," "cares more for others than for self," "doesn't want what it doesn't have," "doesn't keep score of . . . sins," "puts up with anything," and "keeps going to the end" (1 Corinthians 13:4-8)? If old age and hard times meant that your partner was no longer attractive and charming, would you still possess an unselfish, unconditional love?

Here's another way to look at it: Is this a person you can choose to love, each day, for the rest of your life? Because love is much more than a romantic feeling that inevitably ebbs and flows over a lifelong relationship. You can decide to always *love* your mate, but there will be times when you won't *like* your mate. Married love is choosing, one day and even one moment at a time, to give your best to that other person no matter what. That's the kind of committed love God wants for your marriage. Don't settle for anything less.

GOD'S ADVICE

God is love. When we take up permanent residence in a life of love, we live in God and God lives in us. This way, love has the run of the house, becomes at home and mature in us.

1 JOHN 4:16-17

Don't run up debts, except for the huge debt of love you owe each other.

ROMANS 13:8

Trust steadily in God, hope unswervingly, love extravagantly. And the best of the three is love.

1 CORINTHIANS 13:13

Don't become partners with those who reject God. How can you make a partnership out of right and wrong? That's not partnership; that's war.

2 CORINTHIANS 6:14

Love never gives up. Love cares more for others than for self. Love doesn't want what it doesn't have. Love doesn't strut, doesn't have a swelled head, doesn't force itself on others, Isn't always "me first," doesn't fly off the handle, doesn't keep score of the sins of others, doesn't revel when others grovel, takes pleasure in the flowering of truth, puts up with anything, trusts God always, always looks for the best, never looks back, but keeps going to the end. Love never dies.

1 CORINTHIANS 13:4-8

Marriage

OWNING MY FAITH

REALITY CHECK

○ What are the qualities that you're looking for in a marriage partner? loving, smart, funny, problem solver, responsible, considerate

○ What are the best qualities that you would bring to a marriage? ~~strikethrough~~ unconditional love, trust, hope, faith

○ Have you been fooled by love before? How? yes, been told that they love me but just want other things.

○ Though Jesus loves us unconditionally, does unconditional love for another human being seem like an impossible ideal? No, just needs a little work.

○ What scares you the most about marriage? Why? Ending up divorced like my parents b/c they fight all the time and rarely agree on anything, esp. love

Prayer

Master, if there is ever a time that I want to make the right decision, it's when I choose the person I will marry. I pray that You will keep my eyes open to Your Word and my heart in tune with Your will when that time comes. Lord, help me to understand what unconditional love really means, and mold me into a person who can offer that kind of love each day for a lifetime. Amen.

PEACE

Why is there so much conflict in the world? What can I do about it?

Sometimes it feels like our world's gone crazy. Governments battle other nations and their own citizens in civil war. Terrorists fly airplanes into skyscrapers and drive bomb-laden trucks into crowded markets. High school students open fire on their classmates with automatic weapons. Men rape women and sexually abuse children. Mothers murder their kids. The insanity never seems to end. Where did all this evil come from?

It's been around since our beginning, when the serpent worked his gift of persuasion on Eve in the garden (see Genesis 3:1-5). *But why*, you ask, *did God create evil?* He didn't. Everything created by God is good. Yet He also bestowed another gift on His creations—the ability to choose. Though God longs for our love and obedience, He doesn't force it from us. Satan is an angel, created for good by God, who chose to turn away. Today, millions more choose to turn away from God and His excellent plans for us. It's a decision that inevitably distorts our minds and hearts, leading us deeper and deeper into selfishness, resentment, lust, and every other kind of sin.

What can we do against so much evil? Remember that your real enemy is not the person standing before you but *the decision to embrace sin*. Fight not with guns or bombs but with God's weapons: truth, righteousness, peace, faith, and salvation (see Ephesians 6:14-17). Be discerning about what is good and what is not and "before you know it the God of peace will come down on Satan with both feet, stomping him into the dirt" (Romans 16:20). There's nothing crazy about that!

GOD'S ADVICE

This is for keeps, a life-or-death fight to the finish against the Devil and all his angels. Be prepared. You're up against far more than you can handle on your own. Take all the help you can get, every weapon God has issued, so that when it's all over but the shouting you'll still be on your feet.

EPHESIANS 6:12-13

Those who make a practice of sin are straight from the Devil, the pioneer in the practice of sin. The Son of God entered the scene to abolish the Devil's ways.

1 JOHN 3:8

Turn your back on evil, work for the good and don't quit.

PSALM 37:27

The wicked commit slow suicide; they waste their lives hating the good.

PSALM 34:21

"If you decide that it's a bad thing to worship GOD, then choose a god you'd rather serve. . . . As for me and my family, we'll worship GOD."

JOSHUA 24:15

Peace

OWNING MY FAITH

REALITY CHECK

○ Why would an all-powerful God, devoted to goodness, allow evil to exist? Why, for instance, didn't He stop the September 11 attack on the World Trade Center?

○ Is evil's grip on the world stronger than ever or do you believe it's always been like this?

○ How can the small decisions we make each day for "good" make a difference in a world full of evil?

○ What Scripture or biblical character most inspires you to do battle for God?

Write and Reflect

Make a list of times in history or in your life that evil seemed to have the upper hand—and how you or others chose to follow God and left the "battlefield" in victory.

FAMILY

I'm finally free! What do I do when my parents won't let go?

No doubt about it, high school graduation is a significant milestone. It signals the end of childhood and the beginning of your independence, the time when you begin to take control of your life. It's exciting as you start making all the big decisions—where you will live, go to school, work, and worship. During this transition, however, you may observe two people who are struggling to keep up with the program: Mom and Dad.

Your new life is a transition for your parents, too. They've probably spent the last eighteen years caring for you, teaching you, loving you, and praying for you as you've grown. It may be hard for them to accept that they're approaching the final "letting go" stage of parenting. If you're living away from home, you may be dealing with frequent phone calls, expectations to continually stay in touch, and comments that seem to express doubt about your judgment. If you're still in the family home the situation may be even more difficult, starting with questions such as "Where are you going?" and "Where have you been?"

Frustrating as that may be, it's still a good idea to cut your parents some slack. Give them some time and they'll probably adjust to the "new" you. You can also try sitting down with them and explaining how you feel. More communication on both ends may be all that's needed to smooth things over. Your first move, however, should be to take the matter to God in prayer. Ask Him how you can honor your parents (Exodus 20:12) while still maintaining your independence. His way will always be the right way.

GOD'S ADVICE

"Honor your father and mother" is the first commandment that has a promise attached to it, namely, "so you will live well and have a long life."

EPHESIANS 6:2-3

May our dependably steady and warmly personal God develop maturity in you so that you get along with each other as well as Jesus gets along with us all.

ROMANS 15:5

"Let me give you a new command: Love one another. In the same way I loved you, you love one another. This is how everyone will recognize that you are my disciples."

JOHN 13:34-35

"I'm sending Elijah the prophet to clear the way for the Big Day of GOD—the decisive Judgment Day! He will convince parents to look after their children and children to look up to their parents."

MALACHI 4:5-6

There's a right time and way for everything.

ECCLESIASTES 8:6

Family

OWNING MY FAITH

REALITY CHECK

○ You're moving on in life—what seems most difficult for your parents to accept about that? Why do you think that is? *Letting me do it for myself. Maybe they don't trust that I can do it.*

○ In what ways can you honor your parents during this new phase of life? *Not getting mad when they are a bit over bearing.*

○ What is the quality of communication between you and your parents? Is there anything you can do to improve that? *Talking about what goes on w/ me. Yes, do it more & keep it up.*

○ If you have siblings, what impact has your new status in life had on your brothers and sisters? ~~They have~~ *He has become almost distant and trying to push me away.*

Prayer

Father, I love my Mom and Dad, but they sometimes act as if I'm still in middle school. I don't want to cut them out of my life—I'd just like them to treat me with a little more respect. Please show me how to handle this situation. Give me patience to wait on them and see things from their point of view. Give me the right words to explain exactly how I feel, and give them understanding when I do. Thank You, God! Amen.

SEX

I've already blown it, so why stop now?

Stephanie never meant for it to happen. She'd planned to stay a virgin until she married. But Josh had joined the marines and was leaving the next week for basic training. Who knew when, or if, she'd see him again? What was supposed to be only a romantic evening together had turned into much more. Now Stephanie felt horrible. She was mad at Josh and hated herself. Why had she been so stupid? On the other hand, it *had* been exciting. Since she'd already blown it anyway, what did it matter? Maybe she'd sleep with Josh again before he left. Stephanie didn't know what to do.

Here's the deal: Regardless of what's happened in

your life, either last year or last night, God desires you, your heart, and your obedience *right now*. No mistake is so terrible that it can't be forgiven (Mark 3:28), and nothing stands in the way between you and a fresh start. You may be like Nicodemus when he was talking to Jesus, wondering how someone can start over in life and be "born again." As Jesus explained, when you give your sins to God and commit your life to Him, you'll still have the same body. Your spirit, however, will be an entirely new creation—a "living spirit" (John 3:6).

Jesus won't hold your mistakes against you. He also doesn't want you to make more as you try to sort things out. During the conversation with Nicodemus, Jesus chided him for being slow to respond: "Instead of facing the evidence and accepting it, you procrastinate with questions" (verse 11). Whether you've lost your virginity or offended God in some other way, don't procrastinate! Go immediately to Him in prayer. He alone has the power to wash away the past and again point you toward a bright future.

GOD'S ADVICE

Run away from infantile indulgence. Run after mature righteousness.

2 TIMOTHY 2:22

We have no one to blame but the leering, seducing flare-up of our own lust. Lust gets pregnant, and has a baby: sin! Sin grows up to adulthood, and becomes a real killer.

JAMES 1:14-15

The earlier troubles are gone and forgotten, banished far from my sight.

ISAIAH 65:16

Our old way of life was nailed to the Cross with Christ, a decisive end to that sin-miserable life—no longer at sin's every beck and call!

ROMANS 6:6

Don't loiter and linger, waiting until the very last minute. Dress yourselves in Christ, and be up and about!

ROMANS 13:14

Sex

OWNING MY FAITH

REALITY CHECK

○ In what ways have you "blown it" with God? How have you usually responded?

○ Why is it hard to keep trying after you've totally messed up?

○ Whether you're a virgin or not, how motivated are you to stay sexually pure from this point forward?

○ Why do you think, if you can still achieve salvation later, that God puts so much importance on a commitment to Christ now?

○ How confident are you that God can truly give you a new, "living spirit"?

The Next Step

Read about the story of David and Bathsheba and its aftermath in 2 Samuel chapters 11 through 18. Do you think God was too easy or too harsh on David? How might things have been different if David, instead of arranging for the death of Bathsheba's husband and marrying her, had immediately confessed his sexual sin to God?

DEPRESSION

I'm drowning. Is there any hope?

It's no secret that depression is a major issue among people in high school and the years immediately following. In the United States, suicide is the third leading cause of death among people ages fifteen to twenty-four.[2] Even those who have discovered the hope of Jesus can be blindsided by the unexpected loss of a loved one, illness, a financial disaster, or simply the overwhelming weight of daily life. At one time or other, it's probably happened to you—that feeling of going under without a life preserver in sight.

Many people who are "drowning" prefer to keep it to themselves. But this isn't the time to be silent—it's a time to yell for help! Choose a trusted friend, family member,

Depression

pastor, professor, physician, or counselor to confide in. Don't worry about looking foolish. Nearly everyone's been there at least once in life. If you think that person isn't taking you seriously, go on to the next one. God designed us to depend on each other in times of need: "It's better to have a partner than to go it alone. Share the work, share the wealth. And if one falls down, the other helps" (Ecclesiastes 4:9-10).

Of course, no one will better understand how you feel — and offer a greater message of hope — than Jesus. He's known despair, as when He cried out on the cross, "My God, my God, why have you abandoned me?" (Matthew 27:46). Yet He also knows that no matter how dark your life seems, victory will ultimately be yours if you trust Him and focus on your future home in the "new Jerusalem" (Revelation 3:12). He's already preparing a place just for you.

GOD'S ADVICE

Wait . . . for GOD. Wait with hope. Hope now; hope always!

PSALM 131:3

"Don't panic. I'm with you. There's no need to fear for I'm your God. I'll give you strength. I'll help you. I'll hold you steady, keep a firm grip on you.

ISAIAH 41:10

"I'm a hostage here for hope, not doom."

ACTS 28:20

We who have run for our very lives to God have every reason to grab the promised hope with both hands and never let go. It's an unbreakable spiritual lifeline, reaching past all appearances right to the very presence of God.

HEBREWS 6:18-19

"I'm on my way; I'll be there soon. Keep a tight grip on what you have so no one distracts you and steals your crown. I'll make each conqueror a pillar in the sanctuary of my God, a permanent position of honor. Then I'll write names on you, the pillars: the Name of my God, the Name of God's City—the new Jerusalem coming down out of Heaven—and my new Name."

REVELATION 3:11-12

Depression

OWNING MY FAITH

REALITY CHECK

○ What or who is most encouraging to you when you're depressed?

○ What's been the lowest point of your life? Were you able to find comfort in God?

○ Why is it harder to trust God when you're down?

○ What do you imagine your heavenly home in the "new Jerusalem" will be like?

Prayer

Master, I don't know why I get so discouraged sometimes. I can't talk, I can't think, I lose my motivation. I find it hard even to talk to You. Yet You are my answer! Lord, though I feel I have nothing to offer, I offer myself to You. Give me hope when I feel hopeless and help when I feel helpless. Fill me with Your Spirit. Show me a picture of what life in the new Jerusalem will be. Throw me a lifeline that leads straight to You. Amen.

TIME

What can I do when 24/7 isn't enough?

For God, time never presents an obstacle. His perspective of time covers eternity. God has "all the time in the world—whether a thousand years or a day, it's all the same" (Psalm 90:4). For the rest of us, however, time can be a bit harder to manage. Especially now that new responsibilities are piling on, you may find it virtually impossible to make it all happen—working, studying, paying bills, shopping for food, clothes, and school supplies. And of course you need your social life! Important things like exercise, sleep, and time with God can begin to fall through the cracks.

If you feel like a victim of your own schedule, it may

Time

be "time" for a little review. Think about how you spend your day — are you devoting minutes or hours to TV, video games, and the Internet? How much time do you spend just talking with friends? Would your studying go twice as fast if you did it with the stereo off? If you really are managing your time well but still can't keep up, maybe you're trying to do too much. See if there's an activity you can live without. And remember — sometimes the best response to a new opportunity is to say "thanks, but no."

Whatever your situation, you know you've got a problem if God is getting squeezed out of your schedule. He's the one who will help you keep life in perspective. Without God, everything else is "smoke, and spitting into the wind" (Ecclesiastes 1:14). Make Him your first priority and you may find the rest of your time taking care of itself.

GOD'S ADVICE

There's a right time and way for everything.

ECCLESIASTES 8:6

Now is the right time to listen, the day to be helped. Don't put it off; don't frustrate God's work by showing up late.

2 CORINTHIANS 6:2-3

Watch your step. Use your head. Make the most of every chance you get. These are desperate times!

EPHESIANS 5:15-16

Sound thinking makes for gracious living.

PROVERBS 13:15

You have bedded me down in lush meadows, you find me quiet pools to drink from. True to your word, you let me catch my breath and send me in the right direction.

PSALM 23:2-3

Time

OWNING MY FAITH

REALITY CHECK

○ Would you say you're managing your schedule well or is your schedule managing you?

○ Are you spending time each day in prayer and studying God's Message?

○ What seems to most easily throw you off your schedule? What can you do about that?

○ Do you have a hard time saying "no" to people?

○ What do you think of people who appear disorganized and are constantly running behind? What does that kind of life say to God?

The Next Step

For the next week, keep track of how you spend your time—how much with God, how much sleeping, how much working, how much listening to music, and so on. At the end of the week, add up your numbers. Any surprises? Think about any changes you'd like to make in the way you live your life.

REMORSE

We went too far . . . and now he/she's gone. Will the guilt ever go away?

Ever heard of a remora? It's a bony marine fish with a unique talent—the ability to attach a small disk on its head to the body of another fish. Some large fish swim around with several of these aquatic nuisances clinging to them and slowing them down wherever they go.

Guilt is like that. It clings to us like a remora, hindering each of us from the life God intends. You may have gone too far sexually with your boyfriend. In anger, you may have said something terrible to your best friend. Maybe you've been cheating on your midterms. There's no sugarcoating it—there *are* unpleasant consequences to sin. But never-ending remorse doesn't have to be one of them. Of all God's gifts to us, forgiveness and grace are among the most renewing and vital to understanding and living the life of a believer.

In a way, guilt is a form of punishing yourself for your mistakes. But judgment is God's department—He's much more qualified than you to decide on the penalties for sin. It's better to confess your mistakes to God, resolve to follow Him, and brush off clinging regrets. Then you can claim the words of Paul as your own: "In a single victorious stroke of Life, all three—sin, guilt, death—are gone, the gift of our Master, Jesus Christ. Thank God!" (1 Corinthians 15:57).

GOD'S ADVICE

Distress that drives us to God [is all gain]. It turns us around. It gets us back in the way of salvation. We never regret that kind of pain. But those who let distress drive them away from God are full of regrets, end up on a deathbed of regrets.

2 CORINTHIANS 7:10

If we admit our sins—make a clean breast of them—he won't let us down; he'll be true to himself. He'll forgive our sins and purge us of all wrongdoing.

1 JOHN 1:9

As far as sunrise is from sunset, he has separated us from our sins.

PSALM 103:12

"Turn to face God so he can wipe away your sins, pour out showers of blessing to refresh you, and send you the Messiah he prepared for you, namely, Jesus."

ACTS 3:19-20

God deals out joy in the present, the *now*. It's useless to brood over how long we might live.

ECCLESIASTES 5:20

You lifted the cloud of guilt from your people, you put their sins far out of sight.

PSALM 85:2

Remorse

OWNING MY FAITH

REALITY CHECK

○ Though it sounds strange, is it possible that you sometimes *want* to hang on to your guilt?

○ Do you fear taking your worst mistakes to God? Would you rather feel guilty than deal with God's justice?

○ Are there mistakes in your life, maybe even years old, that you've never confessed to God? Can you ask for forgiveness now?

○ Have you ever repented before God and still kept the guilt? Why?

Prayer

Dear God, I'm so sorry for all of the stupid things I've done in my life. Despite Your love and guidance, I seem to make the same mistakes again and again, and in the process make myself more and more miserable. Help me to give all of that to You, and to accept Your grace and cleansing forgiveness. I want to start over with only the joy of Jesus in my heart. Amen.

LONELINESS

I feel abandoned and alone. Now what?

Remember the movie *Cast Away?* Tom Hanks plays a FedEx employee who's stranded for four years on a deserted island. Once Tom figures out how to provide the physical elements he needs to survive — food, water, shelter, and fire — he faces a much harder test: loneliness. His days are marked by increasing anguish and desperation. Finally, to keep his sanity, he creates an unusual companion — a volleyball, appropriately named "Wilson."

Sometimes, life after high school feels like being stranded on a deserted island. It may be that everything you've known has been stripped away. You're in new surroundings with new responsibilities, and you may be miles from family or a true friend. Or you may be around friends constantly, yet still feel disconnected and lonely.

God knows about your need for true companionship. After all, He's the one who said, "It's not good for the Man to be alone" (Genesis 2:18). Though it probably doesn't feel like it, your loneliness may actually be an opportunity. God longs to be the one to fill your desire for deeper relationship (Psalm 91:14). He is there in your loneliness. He wants to be there for you. Reach out to Him with praise and prayer, and He will respond. His promise is that He'll always be with you, "day after day after day, right up to the end of the age" (Matthew 28:20).

GOD'S ADVICE

GOD will never walk away from his people, never desert his precious people.

PSALM 94:14

"If anyone loves me, he will carefully keep my word and my Father will love him—we'll move right into the neighborhood!"

JOHN 14:23

GOD, your God, is above all a compassionate God. In the end he will not abandon you, he won't bring you to ruin, he won't forget the covenant with your ancestors which he swore to them.

DEUTERONOMY 4:31

"If you'll hold on to me for dear life," says GOD, "I'll get you out of trouble. I'll give you the best of care if you'll only get to know and trust me. Call me and I'll answer, be at your side in bad times; I'll rescue you, then throw you a party. I'll give you a long life, give you a long drink of salvation!"

PSALM 91:14-16

Loneliness

OWNING MY FAITH

REALITY CHECK

 Do you get stressed when you're alone or do you enjoy periods of solitude?

Do you get stressed when you're alone or do you enjoy periods of solitude?

When in your life were you most lonely? How did that change?

Do you think there is ever a purpose for your loneliness?

Whom do you usually turn to when you're lonely? Why?

The Next Step

Schedule a time in the next forty-eight hours to reach out to someone who might be lonely or need a friend. *Also,* schedule a quiet time in the next twenty-four hours to just be in God's presence.

TROUBLES

My life keeps falling apart.
Will this ever end?

We all face hard times in our lives. Now that you're out in the world, exploring new opportunities and taking more chances, you're more likely than ever to encounter trials—the death of someone close to you, the breakup of an important relationship, unexpected battles with your roommate, whatever it may be. Most of us choose fairly common methods to deal with our difficulties. We take time to grieve. We ask ourselves what went wrong. We look for a new roommate. Few of us, though, embrace a biblical strategy that could be paraphrased as "Bring it on!"

For instance, James, brother of Jesus, considered it a "gift" when troubles arrived in waves. Peter, leader of the disciples, wrote that believers should be "glad" when they are immersed in the kind of suffering that Christ experienced. And the apostle Paul said that we should "shout our praise" when we're surrounded by hardship. How can oppression be seen as opportunity? Because adversity, according to James, develops and matures our faith. Because suffering, said Peter, refines our spirit and brings us closer to God's glory. Because troubles, explained Paul, lead to patience, virtue, and greater awareness of God's will. But that doesn't mean the pain is softened.

Have no doubt—your difficulty is temporary. If you trust Him, God will rescue you from your crisis at the proper time (see Psalm 91:14-16; 2 Peter 2:9). He knows exactly what He's doing. In the meantime, consider the benefits of your situation. As your faith deepens, you may even find the strength to say "Bring it on!" when your struggles mean greater glory for the Master.

GOD'S ADVICE

Consider it a sheer gift, friends, when tests and challenges come at you from all sides. You know that under pressure, your faith-life is forced into the open and shows its true colors. So don't try to get out of anything prematurely. Let it do its work so you become mature and well-developed, not deficient in any way.

JAMES 1:2-4

We continue to shout our praise even when we're hemmed in with troubles, because we know how troubles can develop passionate patience in us, and how that patience in turn forges the tempered steel of virtue, keeping us alert for whatever God will do next.

ROMANS 5:3-4

Those who wait upon GOD get fresh strength. They spread their wings and soar like eagles.

ISAIAH 40:31

If you're abused because of Christ, count yourself fortunate. It's the Spirit of God and his glory in you that brought you to the notice of others.

1 PETER 4:14

God is a safe place to hide, ready to help when we need him.

PSALM 46:1

Pure gold put in the fire comes out of it *proved* pure; genuine faith put through this suffering comes out *proved* genuine.

1 PETER 1:7

Troubles

OWNING MY FAITH

REALITY CHECK

◯ Does your life seem to be falling apart? Is that due to external circumstances or your own doing?

◯ Are your current troubles developing your patience and maturing your faith? Why or why not?

◯ Could God have found a better way to refine our spirits?

◯ When have you noticed spiritual benefits from trials in your life?

Write and Reflect

Write out in longhand all of Psalm 91, then memorize verses 14 through 16. Reflect on what this Scripture means to you as a child of God.

CONFUSION

What do I do when I don't know what to do?

It's exciting to be on your own for the first time—but let's face it, it can also be bewildering. You're constantly making decisions that may affect your future for months and years to come—where to live and whom to live with, what classes to take, whom or whether to date, and can you afford that new laptop? And unlike your friend down the hall who seems to have it all together, you're getting more and more confused. Deep down, you're not really sure who you are. You might even be feeling uncertain about God and where you stand spiritually.

Understand that it's okay to feel confused. This is a time in life for testing and exploring. You'll emerge from all this uncertainty with a better feeling for yourself, your strengths and weaknesses, your passions, and your values. If you give Him a chance, you'll also come away with a better understanding of God. The key is to allow Him time to reveal Himself to you. A period of confusion is actually a great opportunity to dig deeper into God's Word and your prayer life.

Remember, even Jesus frequently withdrew from teaching and making miracles so that He could be alone to pray (see Matthew 14:23; Mark 1:35; Luke 5:15-16). If Christ, who could do anything, often sought rest and renewal with the Father, how much more do we need the same? Let the Lord show you the way. He won't turn on a floodlight to illuminate the entire landscape, but He will "throw a beam of light" (Psalm 119:105) to reveal your next step. When He's the one leading, that's enough.

GOD'S ADVICE

Trust GOD from the bottom of your heart; don't try to figure out everything on your own. Listen for GOD's voice in everything you do, everywhere you go; he's the one who will keep you on track.

PROVERBS 3:5-6

When we worship the right way, God doesn't stir us up into confusion; he brings us into harmony.

1 CORINTHIANS 14:33

Stalwart walks in step with GOD; his path blazed by GOD, he's happy.

PSALM 37:23

"The Friend, the Holy Spirit whom the Father will send at my request, will make everything plain to you. He will remind you of all the things I have told you."

JOHN 14:26

For those who love what you reveal, everything fits — no stumbling around in the dark for them.

PSALM 119:165

Cry for help and you'll find it's grace and more grace. . . . Your teacher will be right there, local and on the job, urging you on whenever you wander left or right: "This is the right road. Walk down this road."

ISAIAH 30:19-21

Confusion

REALITY CHECK

◯ What's most confusing in your life right now? What are the things that you can count on?

◯ Do you sense that God is guiding your life today or does He seem to be "missing in action"?

◯ Are you listening for God's voice?

◯ Is busyness a source of your confusion? Do you ever stop to rest and renew?

◯ What would your life look like without confusion? What do you need to do for that to happen?

Prayer

Father, it's all too much—too many choices, too many people and ideas that just don't make sense to me. I confess that sometimes I feel I don't understand You, either. Yet I sense the love and truth behind Your Message, and I know that the more I pursue You, the more I'll find clarity and peace. Dear God, calm my heart and show me the direction to go so that I can always follow You. Thank You so much for Your unfailing love for me. Amen.

NOTES

1. **Obedience:** Illustration adapted from Rolf Zettersten, *Dr. Dobson: Turning Hearts Toward Home* (Dallas: Word Publishing, 1989), pp. 13-17.
2. **Depression:** Suicide statistic from US Centers for Disease Control and Prevention, http://www.cdc.gov/ncipc/factsheets/suifacts.htm.

READ HIS STORY LIKE NEVER BEFORE WITH

The Message Remix

God's Word was meant to be read. But more than that, it was meant to be understood. It was first written in the language of the people—of fishermen, shopkeepers, and carpenters. *The Message Remix* gets back to that: you can read it and understand it.

In *The Message Remix*, there are verse-numbered paragraphs that will help you study and find favorite passages. Or you can just read it like a book and let the narrative speak to you. After all, it is God's story, with its heroes and villains, conflicts and resolutions. Either way, it's God's Word—the truth—in a user-friendly form.

To order copies, visit your local Christian bookstore, call NavPress at 1-800-366-7788, or log on to www.navpress.com.

To locate a Christian bookstore near you, call 1-800-991-7747.